Resolving Conflict God's Way

Listening to God Whenever Conflict Arises

JERRY AND CAROLE WILKINS

Copyright © 2015 Jerry and Carole Wilkins
All rights reserved
First Edition

PAGE PUBLISHING, INC.
New York, NY

First originally published by Page Publishing, Inc. 2015

ISBN 978-1-68213-590-7 (pbk)
ISBN 978-1-68213-591-4 (digital)
ISBN 978-1-68213-592-1 (hardcover)

Printed in the United States of America

Contents

Introduction..5

God Says God Says Always Speak the Truth in Love......................11

God Says God Says Always Be Kind to Others 16

God Says We Are to Cease from Anger..19

God Says Disagreeing in the Christian Way................................23

God Says Resist the Urge to Retaliate or Get Back at Someone 27

God Says We Are To Work toward Peace......................................30

God Says Recognize the Role Satan Plays in Conflict 33

God Says Judging Others Is Wrong and Forbidden 36

God Says Be Tolerant of Differences..39

God Says Forgive Those Who Wrong You in Conflict 42

God Says God Forbids Malice and Bitterness 46

God Says Patience Is God's Way, Even in Conflict..........................49

God Says The Greatest of these is Love 52

God Says We Are to Safeguard Unity and Oneness.......................56

God Says Observe All God's Submission Principles 60

God Says We Are To Think the Best of Others...............................67

God Says God Says Love Even Your Enemy 70

God Says Exhibit Self-control in Conflict...73

God Says God Says We Should Live Unselfishly............................77

Conclusion...81

Appendix 1 My Marriage Conflict Covenant.................................83

Appendix 2 My Church Conflict Covenant....................................84

Appendix 3 My Workplace Conflict Covenant..............................85

Appendix 4 God's Word on Conflict 86

Introduction

Conflict is inevitable. Everyone experiences conflict from time to time. Conflict is indeed a fact of life. Wherever two or more people are found together, in your home, in your church, in your workplace, in your extended family, there is the potential for conflict. Conflict can be defined in many ways. Conflict can be called a struggle, a battle, a clash of ideas and opinions. It can range from everyday "verbal push and pull" to the extreme of "doing whatever is necessary to triumph over someone or something." Other words for conflict could include confrontations, disagreements, discord, friction, and arguments. Personal conflict is when two or more people engage in opposing positions, struggling for dominance. God wants to be involved in all our conflicts but this book is about how we shut Him out of our conflicts.

Conflict can happen in the marriage relationship, resulting in misery or divorce. Few, if any, marriages are devoid of conflict. Thousands of marriages end painfully for not only husband and wife, but also for the children and the extended family. Two people come together in marriage so passionately in love that nothing else matters. Then as they live in the same house or apartment twelve hours every day for three-hundred-sixty-five days every year, the different opinions and habits begin to take their toll. Conflict is the natural result, and it is a tribute to love and commitment that so many marriages endure for life. This success rate would greatly increase if couples would manage and resolve conflict God's way.

Conflict can also happen in a friendship or simple relationship, sometimes resulting in heated hatred or even murder. So many friends part ways because neither friend can manage and resolve a conflict of ideas or interest. A single conflict can erase dozens of years of friendship. Casual simple relationships between neighbors can disappear over mismanaged conflict. The friendships we develop at places where we eat out, places where we buy our food and clothes, and even gas, can all be destroyed because of conflict where people don't know how to bring about acceptable resolution. *Or maybe they know how, but choose to ignore the how because the inner pressure to be right and to win is so great.*

Conflict can occur at work. Forty to fifty hours a week can be a long time together in the close confines and relentless pressures of everyday working together. The competition to get ahead and climb the ladder can be fertile ground for conflict. The addition of mediators and arbitrators is often not enough to settle the conflict on the personal level and the conflict does its damage to the personal friendships.

As a minister, I feel the greatest possibility for conflict is in the local church arena, second only to the marriage arena. Dozens, hundreds, even thousands of people from every walk of life come together several times each week for worship, Bible classes, and fellowship. In addition to that, many of these church members serve alongside each other in ministries, on committees, and in church organizations. The different backgrounds and the diversity make this crowd of Christians easy to have differences and engage in conflict. Every church I served had conflicts arise. Most of the conflicts related to the personal preferences of members. Some liked traditional worship, and others wanted to have contemporary worship. Some of the conflicts had to do with the music style. In the denominational news, we heard talk of "music wars" or "worship wars." Other conflicts revolved around church budgets and the things the church spent money on. I remember conflict over the amount the church budgeted for missionary support. Another was over how we chose our deacons and who was qualified to serve as a deacon. It seems when you have so many people, you also have so many ideas and opinions. Unless a wise leader can rightly manage these conflicts, they can do a lot of damage to the fellowship. Church conflicts that are not managed well can cause a pastor or other staff minister to resign or be fired; other damage involves the loss of members. In worse cases, churches split or close because of mismanaged conflict.

Conflict arises in school, in a civic group, or in different government levels, local, county, state, and national. We've all laughed at the news or *Youtube* videos of government leaders jumping on each other or slugging each other all around the world. Conflicts can happen between nations and result in devastating wars with the loss of thousands, even millions of lives. Simply put, conflict is found everywhere. God's Word says man's days are few and full of trouble, and much of that trouble comes in the form of conflict.

The purpose of this book is not to address the times in life when conflict is necessity and even justified, for example war or national defense, but to help each of us deal with the everyday conflicts that arise. **This is not a book about what I think, but what God actually says about conflict and how we manage it.** Our commentary is an attempt at helping people understand what God is saying in His word and how they can apply His words in their times of conflict. Therefore, a great deal of space is given to the actual words of God, rather than ours.

Most of us realize how much harm personal conflict can cause if not managed correctly. Rather than being ignorant of God's Word, or ignoring or forgetting to apply His words at a time of conflict, we must learn to apply His words. Tossing God's words to the side while we handle conflict is equated to not calling the fire department when there's a fire or not going to the doctor when we're sick. The damage to relationships, marriages, families, financial security, or church unity is devastating. The scourge of conflict is everywhere, and wrecked lives are testimony to conflict's destructive power. The damage can last for years, and some people carry the hurt and wreckage around for a lifetime, many times because we don't involve God in our management and resolution.

Our objective is to address "personal conflict." Everyone involved in conflict thinks and feels they are right, that their way should prevail. But how can we really know who is right? After a lifetime of observing conflict, we believe there are often good people on both sides of the conflict or the disagreement. People in conflict with us are not always evil people. People may be misguided, confused, even self-centered; but they can also be good people.

There is, of course, evil in the world, and sometimes that evil is being expressed in the form of personal conflicts. But it is counter-productive to assign all personal conflict to the eternal battle between good and evil, right and wrong. We should resist the natural tendency to demonize everyone who opposes or disagrees with us. This is especially true in the area of church conflicts.

My wife and I have worked together on this book to help people manage conflict by applying God's instructions to personal conflict whenever and wherever it occurs. My wife of forty-eight years, a trained counselor who has counseled hundreds of people in conflict, has had a lot of experiences counseling people with relationship conflicts. She has guided me as I applied the words of God to real life situations. Though I did a lot of counseling as a pastor and as a denominational leader, my main contribution is in searching God's Word and applying it to life situations.

As we said, in the heat of conflict, we tend to forget to listen to God. We might say God is the great "conflict buster" and the one we should all call on to have victory over conflict in God's way. Victory over the conflict is not the same as victory in the conflict, or victory over the opposition. Victory over the conflict comes when the conflict is resolved.

But we don't call on or turn to God's Word when conflict raises its ugly head. This is why conflict is so rampant, and why it escalates so easily. This is why there are so many divorces, church splits, job related shootings, instances of road rage, and other conflicted situations. We forget or we ignore all we know of God's Word when we engage in conflict. It is as if we tell God to go away for a time while we handle the conflict. We act as if we have thrown God's directions, God's Word, out the window. His instructions are unknown, forgotten, or ignored. What we need is intervention, a God intervention. Something is too often missing when conflict arises. What's missing is God! What we need is to hear a "word from God." God has a lot to say about conflict and how we should manage and resolve conflict. He has a lot to say about how we should act during conflict. We must obey all of God's commands even when we are seeking to win in a conflict.

God may or may not give us the answer to the conflict, but He will surely direct the way we act, the way we react, the way we speak, and what we say in the conflict. Hearing from Him will keep us from managing conflict in the "flesh." This is what spirals conflict out of control and makes conflict so destructive. Conflict without God is a recipe for damage, pain, and even disaster.

So let's look together at the "Words of God" that apply to how we manage ourselves when we are in conflict. Let's internalize these words from God, hiding them in our heart and mind, so they influence how we manage personal conflict, whether at home, at work, at church, or elsewhere.

A word of caution: Let's be careful to apply these Words from God to ourselves and avoid the urge to apply them only to the other person. We can find ourselves using these words to take shots at the opposition. Let's trust that God will apply these words to the opposition in His own time and in His own way. The only thing we can change is the way we manage conflict personally. Rather, let's apply God's directions to the words, actions, reactions, and even the thoughts we have when we are engaged in conflict. By doing it God's way, we may have the only real chance of being truly "right" in any conflict. So after you read this book or study it in your church, we hope you'll know who to call when conflict arises. Call the conflict buster, God Himself.

We have filled this book with the Words of God because we want you to hear from Him and understand what He says about how you handle conflict. For this reason, we have put His Words in *italics. Other words are ours as we try to help you understand His words more fully.* I have used the Kings James Version of the Bible which is acceptable to most Christians. Most Christians read other translations which provide more up to date translation. If I use other translations, it is to make the meaning more understandable to the present day use of the English language. I also place in (parentheses) words we add in the scripture to help you better understand words and apply the intent of the verse. Our promise to you is that we take God's words very seriously and give great effort to translating correctly into terms you can understand. So let's get started listening to what God has to say about how we handle conflict. Appling these words to what you do, what you say, and how you say it can change your whole life. Let these words be the protecting warning about the things you should not do when you find yourself in conflict.

Word One

God Says Always Speak the Truth in Love

Eph. 4:15a *But, SPEAKING the truth in love, may grow up into Him in all things.*

Prov. 6:16–17 *These six things doth the Lord hate: Yea, seven are an abomination* (extreme disgust and hatred) *unto him: A proud look, a lying tongue…a false witness that speaketh lies, and he that soweth discord among brethren.*

Prov. 10:18 *He that hideth hatred with lying lips, and he that uttereth a SLANDER, is a fool.*

Prov. 12:22 *Lying lips are abomination to the Lord, but they that deal truly are his delight.*

1 Tim. 3:11 *Even so must their wives* (deacon's wives) *be grave* (serious), *not SLANDERERS.*

1 Pet. 2:1 *Wherefore laying aside all malice, and all GUILE, and hypocrisies, and envies, and all evil speakings.*

1 Pet. 2:22 *Who (Christ who also suffered) did no sin, neither was GUILE found in his mouth:*

1 Pet. 3:10 *For he that will love life, and see good days, let him refrain his tongue from evil, and his lips that they speak no GUILE:*

Author's Commentary

These "words" of God apply at all times, even when we are in some type conflict. First, the Word of God commands us to tell the truth, always. Guile is deceitfulness. Telling the truth is always in order, although it may not always be necessary or beneficial. God does not ask us to withhold the truth. It is important that the real truth "stand up" and be heard. It is okay to be assertive in that you tell what you sincerely know to be the truth. To be faithful to God's commands does not require that we hide or even withhold the truth as we know it. It is important that people who know the truth share that truth if the sharing would be beneficial and productive. We will share later that we need to always confirm in our mind that the sharing will indeed be beneficial. I have often heard someone tell the truth, and the telling greatly hurt someone. At the same time, there was no need to tell the truth, and the telling was no more than the teller stroking his or her ego or pride. We will expand on this as we talk about *motive* later in the section.

But secondly, even though telling the truth is permitted and even important in some cases, caution is in order here. We must tell *only the truth*. We must not knowingly tell an untruth, or something we only heard to be the truth, not knowing it is truth for sure. God has said much about the sin of lying, especially when the lie is gossip, slander, or guile about another person. We must not tell gossip as the truth. We must avoid telling as the truth something we only think to be the truth. For example, we think someone broke into a neighbor's house because you've always thought that person was dishonest. This issue of truth, gossip, and motive for communicating is more true today with the appearance of "social media" with its Facebook, Twitter, blogs, and so many more ways to tell stuff about others without being identified yourself. But the truth may not be the same as our opinion. Tell only what you know, *really know* to be the truth.

Here's another example. We may be tempted to tell what we think is someone's motive in doing something or saying something. In truth, we can only conjecture or guess that this is the truth. We cannot know for sure "why" a person does something. This is true all the way from the White House to your house and even in God's house, the local church. The truth may be we are right or we could be wrong. This is especially true when we are engaged in some type of conflict. Speak the truth, but only the truth, when in conflict. Too often we jump to saying or telling something that is not true or something we cannot be sure is the truth. If I say to my spouse or to anyone for that matter, "You always..." or "You never..." this may be my perception but not really the truth. Too often, when we are in conflict with someone we are tempted to tell a half truth. I remember a minister and his wife who had been accused of imposing on a church member, using and wearing out the member's washing machine. The member was in conflict with the minister after a period of friendship. The member was saying the minister and his wife just assumed they could come over with their wash and borrow the machine. The member was telling a half-truth all over the church and all over the small town. The full truth was the member and his wife had offered the use of the machine once a week. When the conflict started, the whole truth was not told. This same member told around the church that the minister's wife wrote all the minister's sermons. This untruth resulted from the minister, upon receiving a compliment on his sermons, joking that they should thank his wife because she did all the sermon writing. It is to our shame if we lie or gossip what we don't know to be the truth just to hurt or damage someone we are in conflict with at the time. God commands us to tell the whole truth even when we are in conflict.

So, when in conflict, we must hear God telling us to be careful that we tell the truth when it is beneficial and helpful, BUT we tell nothing but the truth. Many conflicts in the home, in the church, or wherever conflict occurs intensify and grow when we forget or ignore God's commands.

At the same time, telling what we know to be the truth does not excuse us from other Christian traits such as kindness, patience, love, and peace. In the Ephesians passage above, God says whenever we tell what we know to be the truth, we tell the truth "in love." Too often, when thinking we are right, we feel justified in being angry, unkind, verbally abusive, impatient, and even war-like. We will see as we hear all God's words I have collected together in the book, these things are never justified, even if we are right. What we say may be true, but it can be dishonored and negated by the way we say it. Say everything in love.

But what does "in love" mean? First, we think it means that the person we are speaking to can, or at least could if they would, sense that we have love in our heart for them. That is the acid test. Does love show through in the way we speak or does hate, or anger, or contempt, or judgment come through louder than love? Love is biblically defined as patient, kind, forgiving, and unselfish (1 Corinthians 13). It should be this love that the opposition senses and observes in our speech as we tell what we honestly know to be the truth. It is not what you say but how you say it that matters. Say everything in love. When you are in conflict, do others hear love mixed in with the truth?

Love should be our manner and our motive. Our motive for our speaking the truth is to be love. Please read the chapter on Love and you will understand better this awesome concept of speaking only the truth in a loving way and with love as your motive.

Later in the book, we will address God's instructions that we first speak the truth to the person we are in conflict with, rather than speaking it to everybody else.

So what have these "words from God" said to us about how we manage conflict? Are we helped by hearing from Him? We are to be willing and free to tell the truth, and only what we know to be the truth, doing it with a loving motive and in a loving manner. What a difference this would make!

Now let's think about how well we followed these directions during any resent conflicts.

Personal Questions to Consider:

Am I willing to speak the truth when it's really necessary?
Do I think about the benefits and the results of speaking the truth before I speak the truth?
Do I know everything I say to others to really be true?
Do I claim I know why someone does something, even though I'm unable to know their true motive?
Are the words I speak acceptable to my Lord?
Would I say what I say if Jesus were standing there with me?
When I speak, do I do it in a loving manner and with the motive of love?

Word Two

God Says Always Be Kind to Others

Eph. 4:32 *And be ye KIND ONE TO ANOTHER, tenderhearted, forgiving one another, even as God for Christ's sake hath forgiven you.*

Rom. 12:10 *Be KINDLY affectioned one to another with brotherly love; in honour preferring one another;*

1 Cor. 13:4 *Charity (Love) suffereth long and is KIND*

Col. 3:12 *Put on therefore, as the elect of God, holy and beloved, bowels of mercies, KINDNESS, humbleness of mind, meekness, longsuffering;*

2 Pet. 1:5–9 *And beside this, giving all diligence, add to your faith virtue; and to virtue knowledge; And to knowledge temperance; and to temperance patience; and to patience godliness; And to godli-*

*ness brotherly **kindness**; and to brotherly **kindness** charity (love).*

Author's Commentary

Although kindness may be hard to define, each of us knows when someone is being kind to us. We also know when someone is being unkind to us. Let's think carefully about how we treat others and speak to others during a time of conflict. We often feel we don't have to be kind to those we feel are against us. But the command to be kind is not cancelled by God or put on hold, just because we are engaged in some level of conflict. Surely God's command to be kind even when in conflict points to His knowledge that unkindness will surely escalate and intensify the conflict.

But again, the question is, "What is kind and what is unkind?" Examples of kindness would include a friendly greeting, a handshake or hug, an inquiry about someone's health or family, a word of congratulation, a compliment, a pleasant conversation, a gift, a positive letter, e-mail, text message, or phone call. Even a sharing of different opinions in a calm, respectful way would be called kind.

You can express these "acts of kindness" even when you are engaged in conflict. We have seen this done many times over the years. We have seen this done in marital conflict, in conflict between members of a church congregation, and in many other conflicted situations. It can be done! We've seen Christians give a friendly greeting to someone they were in direct conflict with at the time. We've seen a handshake given to a member of the opposition. There is a power available to us that can make this kindness possible, even toward who are in conflict with us. We are reminded that our Lord said we haven't done anything exceptional when we are kind to those who are kind to us, or to love those who love us. It is admirable and exceptional in the Lord's eyes if we can be kind to those who are not kind to us.

Examples of unkindness would include a refusal to shake hands or acknowledge a person by eye contact, an unkind accusation, the raising of voice, a harsh criticism, or the silent treatment. Again, we all know when we are being treated unkindly. Let's be honest; each of us knows when we are being unkind to someone. It's not an accident. We have seen all these unkind expressions by Christians in conflict.

So if conflict arises, we should call on the Lord and first remember His teachings and then apply those teachings to the way we engage in conflict. Resist the urge to "toss" God's commands just because you are in a time of conflict. Don't conveniently forget that God tells us to be kind always and to everyone. These personal questions will help you think about your willingness to be kind in conflict.

Personal Questions to Consider:

Have I said words to others that I would consider unkind if these words were said to me?
Is my love for my opposition characterized by kindness in words and actions?
Do I refuse to say hello to or shake the hand of someone I consider my opposition in conflict?
Am I kind to those with who I am in conflict?

Word Three

We Are to Cease from Anger

Prov. 15:1 *A soft answer turneth away wrath: but grievous words stir up ANGER.*

Prov. 15:18 *A wrathful man stirreth up strife: but he that is slow to ANGER appeaseth strife.*

Prov. 16:32 *He that is slow to ANGER is better than the mighty; and he that ruleth (controls) his spirit (himself) than he that taketh a city.*

Prov. 19:11 *The discretion (wisdom) of a man deferreth (sets aside) his ANGER; and it is his glory to pass over a transgression (wrong done him).*

Matt. 5:22 *But I say unto you, That whosoever is ANGRY with his brother without a cause shall be in danger of the judgment (*'cause here can mean "truly right reason," not just any cause*).*

Eph. 4:31 *Let all bitterness, and wrath, and ANGER, and clamour, and evil speaking, be put away from you, with all malice:*

Col. 3:8 *But now ye also put off all these; ANGER, wrath, malice, blasphemy, filthy communication out of your mouth.* (Isn't it interesting that the anger mentioned in the last two passages is NOT treated differently than the other sinful actions. This anger is also sinful! To justify our human anger by saying the sinless Jesus got angry fails to hold logic when we read these verses. We believe whatever Jesus felt or displayed was not the human anger we express and is mentioned here as sin. How can we honestly count all the things mentioned here as sinful and neglect to classify our human anger also as sin? Think about it!)

Prov. 14:17 *He that is soon ANGRY deals foolishly:*

Prov. 21:19 *It is better to dwell in the wilderness, than with a contentious* (argumentative) *and an ANGRY woman.*

Prov. 22:24 *Make no friendship with an ANGRY man; and with a furious* (highly angry) *man thou shalt not go*

Prov. 29:22 *An ANGRY man stirreth up strife, and furious man aboundeth in transgression.*

Eph. 4:26 *Be ye ANGRY, and sin not: let not the sun go down upon your wrath:* (Could this mean anger is an emotion like lust, when you realize it's there, you should remove it quickly before it becomes sinful.)

Titus 1:7 *For a bishop* (pastor or minister) *must be blameless, as the steward of God; not self-willed,* *not soon ANGRY...no striker* (not a person who hits others);

Author's Commentary

It is difficult to find a good word about human anger in the Word of God. After a long hard search of scripture, I'm not able to agree that there is any "good anger" humanly speaking. We are never encouraged to be angry, but as the above scriptures show, we are commanded to avoid anger, to cease from anger and remove it from our lives. The harboring of angry feelings never helps in a conflict, and angry outbursts always make conflict worse.

We are all human, and there will be times we feel angry. It sneaks up on us. This is just one sinful human response to external stimulus, and it may be much like lust and envy. These sinful emotions show up without being pre-meditated. But God's Word says we are to put all these aside and rise above the human to the spiritual level of living. To be angry is to live in the flesh; to resist anger is to live in the spirit.

How quick are you to get angry? God says we are to be slow to get angry, and He praises the person who is slow to get angry. How short is your fuse? These passages of God's Word put great value on keeping your cool even when you are in conflict. Conflict for the Christian should not require anger.

If you doubt anger is wrong, even sinful, notice how it is grouped in scriptures above with other sinful traits such as bitterness, wrath, evil speaking, malice, filthy communication, blasphemy, and the like. Some, in an attempt to justify anger, say Jesus was angry in the temple, therefore it is okay for us to get angry. But it cannot be the same thing, the same anger, or Jesus would be guilty of sin, which we know He was not. Whatever Jesus expressed in the temple was something other than the human anger we are talking about and so often express when in conflict. Maybe I chose to say He was being assertive, and his actions of turning over tables and cracking the whip could all have been done without Jesus crossing the line into the anger we are told to avoid. Another option would be to realize Jesus, being God, can express Godly anger without it being sin, but *we cannot*. Even if we believe we are right in the conflict, and who does not think they are right when engaged in conflict, it does not free us from these commands about anger.

If we feel anger rising up in us, we should remove ourselves from the scene or stay in control of our emotions, resisting a show of anger. Self-control is one important fruit of the Spirit (Galatians 5:23 where KJV temperance means self-control in the life of a Christian). The presence of the Holy Spirit and our submission to Him produce self-control in our lives, even when we are in conflict.

God also says we should avoid angry people. Rather than spending time with other angry people and feeding on the anger they exhibit, we should stand against anger by openly rejecting their life choices. This is true especially in the church or work setting. Too often we seek the companionship of other angry people to help our cause in the conflict instead of dealing with only the person we are in conflict with, as Jesus commanded.

So, let's look at some personal questions we should answer honestly, as to whether conflict results in anger in each of us.

Personal Questions to Consider:

Am I angry in any stage of the conflict I am involved in?
How would an honest friend say I should answer this first question?
Am I willing to put away my anger when I feel it?
Do I respond softly when others speak harshly to me?
Do I stay in control of my temper?
Do I stir conflict or do I try to reduce and calm conflict?
Does my anger keep me from overlooking the wrongs done me by others?
Does my anger cause me to speak evil (say bad things) about others?
Am I spending time with angry people?

Word Four

Disagreeing in the Christian Way

I Cor. 3:3 *For ye are yet carnal, for whereas there is among you envying, and strife, and divisions, are ye not carnal, and walk as men?*

1 Cor. 14:40 *Let all things be done DECENTLY and in order.*

1 Cor. 13:5 *Charity (love)…Doth not behave itself unseemly, seeketh not her own, is not easily provoked, thinketh no evil;*

Gal. 5:22–23 *But the fruit of the Spirit is love, joy, peace, longsuffering, gentleness, goodness, faith, meekness, temperance* (self-control: a Christian should always be in control of actions and words).

Matt. 18:15 *Moreover if thy brother shall trespass against thee, go and tell him his fault between thee and him alone.*

James 4:1 *From whence come wars and FIGHTINGS among you? Come they not hence, even of your lusts (*desires*) that war in your members (*within you*)?*

1 Cor. 14:33 *For God is not the author of confusion, but of PEACE.*

1 Tim. 5:1 *REBUKE (scold, berate, or chew out) NOT an elder, BUT ENTREAT him as a father; and the younger men as brothers. And older women as mothers and younger women as sisters. (Our respect for others is important to God).*

Author's Commentary

When in conflict, disagreeing with others, it is important we do so in a Christian way. The Christian way of life is not to be put aside just because a Christian is involved in conflict. Often, conflict is made worse when Christians act in a manner that is selfish, judgmental, angry, out-of-control, and unwilling to seek a peaceful resolution to a problem. Whether in your marriage, in a family gathering, your workplace, your neighborhood, or your church, it is God's will that we act in the way He has set forth for us.

Let's look at the Christian way of disagreeing mentioned in the passages above. I'll try to summarize all of the passages above.

God's Word says that strife and divisions show we are carnal, and acting in the flesh. Isn't it easy to get in the flesh when our way feels threatened. Our spiritual side is overcome by our sinful side. The new man is pushed aside by that old man and his sinful ways. Too often, in our attempt to be right, we act in the wrong ways. Even if we are on the right side of the conflict, our rightness is clouded and obscured by our wrongness.

When a Christian engages in conflict, it should always be done in a decent or respectful way. The Scripture tells us to always be peaceful and to seek peace in every situation. We must resist the urge to act or react in the flesh. This is the old way we used to act before we knew Jesus. Now, we are the peacemakers we will talk about in a later section.

This doesn't mean we cannot express our opinion or state the truth as we perceive it. It simply means we should do it in the Christian way. How you say something is as important as what you say. At times your actions, and the way you state your case, are so loud people cannot hear the content of your argument. In a marital conflict, the way you speak can totally shut down any chance of resolution, compromise, or reconciliation. This truth applies elsewhere also.

Also, when in conflict with someone, we should address the disagreement privately. We are to first talk only with the person we are in conflict with (not talk with family members, friends, other church members, co-workers, etc.). The Christian way is to address the conflict with the person we have disagreement with, seeking a solution. If that does not work, we then involve another wise person or two, seeking their help in resolving the conflict. We believe God knows it best when we involve the smallest number of people as possible, rather than spread the conflict to many others. When will we realize God's way is best and do things his way?

When we make accusations, we should be careful to be calm and respectful (decently). Even if we're accusing someone of wrong, our heart should be broken over that wrong.

The following things are very important, and we believe go along with the intent of the passages above. We should be careful not to interrupt others when they are speaking. We do not talk while others are talking. It is important that Christians learn to listen, especially when in conflict. Even when we disagree, we should be seeking to hear and understand the position of those with whom we are in conflict. We should be listening, not thinking about what we are going to say next. We are to seek to understand other views, even the views of those who oppose us.

God also says we are not to be selfish, wanting our way only. We are to be willing to let the other persons have it their way at times. It seems that God not only says it is more blessed to give, BUT it is more blessed to "give in," also. WOW! How many marriages would be saved, how many churches would avoid splitting, how many jobs would be kept if we would heed these words!

God also tells us of the importance of self-control. Conflict of any kind escalates whenever people choose to lose control. We say choose because it is a choice. You can choose to stay in control of your words and actions. Otherwise, you have chosen to lose control. This loss of control may be observed in the raising of your voice or the swinging of your fists or the slamming of a door, etc. It could be the storming out of the room or the throwing of an object. We've seen each of these as we watched people chose not to control themselves.

Handling conflict in a Christian way is not easy. Becoming a Christian may be easy and free, but living the Christian way is not easy. The Christian way is the hard way but the better way, the most beneficial way. Whether the conflict is with our spouse, a friend, a co-worker, a family member, or a fellow church member, we are called on by God to disagree in a Christian manner and to handle conflict His way.

Personal Questions to Consider:

When in conflict, do I keep it as private as possible?
When I disagree with others, do I look for ways to make peace, rather than win the battle?
When I disagree with others, do I create confusion?
When I disagree with others, do I stay in control of my emotions, my words, and my actions?
When I disagree with others, do I conduct myself decently and in an orderly way?
When I disagree with others, do I give myself over to expressions of anger?
Am I always determined to have things my way?
How would others say I should answer these questions?

Word Five

Resist the Urge to Retaliate or Get Back at Someone

Rom. 12:19 *Avenge not yourselves, but rather give place unto wrath: for it is written, Vengeance is mine; I will repay, saith the Lord.*

Heb. 10:30 *For we know him that hath said, VENGEANCE belongeth unto me, I will recompense, saith the Lord. And again, The Lord shall judge his people.*

1 Cor. 13:5 *Love…thinketh no evil;* (keeps no record of evil done to you)

1 Pet. 2:23 *Who, when he was reviled, reviled not again; when he suffered, he threatened not; but committed himself to him that judgeth righteously.*

1 Cor. 6:7 *Now therefore there is utterly a fault among you, because ye go to law with one another. Why do you not rather take wrong? Why do you not rather suffer yourselves to be defrauded?*

Matt. 5:38–41 *Ye have heard it hath been said, An eye for an eye and a tooth for a tooth: But I say unto you, that ye resist not evil: but whosoever shall smite thee on the right cheek, turn to him the other also. And if any man will sue thee at the law, and take away your coat, let him have your cloak also. And whosoever shall compel thee to go a mile, go with him twain.*

Author's Commentary

One great problem we face when we are managing conflict is the "tit for tat" urge. This is the urge to return hurt for hurt, hit for hit, and pain for pain. It is human nature to want to get back at somebody when they have hurt you in some way. And more often than not, conflict usually results in someone feeling hurt. Conflict involves winners and losers, and it hurts to be a loser. Conflict usually involves someone not getting their way, and not getting your way causes pain for most of us. This is true whether the hurt is at the office, in the home, or at your church. So conflicts result most often in someone feeling threatened by hurt or actually being hurt as the result of the conflict. This triggers our urge to hurt back.

This desire to retaliate or have revenge is normal to the "natural" or "carnal" person. Our "old" nature is controlled by our flesh, and our fleshly nature demands we get back at those who hurt us. We can take revenge in a multitude of ways. In extreme, it can be done with physical violence. More often in modern times it is through other means. We may seek to do damage through hurtful words. It may be the absence of words, or the silent treatment. Refusal to talk to those we are in conflict with is a common strategy for revenge. The refusal to return a greeting given us or respond to an outstretched hand is another way to hurt back.

It is important to remember that Christians are not to let evil done to them register or be remembered. We keep no record of the harm or hurt others do us. This in itself rules out any desire to get back at someone. This supports the words of our Lord saying we should not retaliate with "eye for eye or tooth for tooth." When a husband and wife are in conflict, the conflict worsens when one of them returns hurt for hurt. It is this urge that keep warring nations or groups fighting. No one is willing to suffer wrong without striking back. This is true in the workplace, in your neighborhood, or in your church and sadly, in a loving marriage too. We are not to return hurt for hurt; rather we are to suffer wrong done us without retaliation. These are not our words or ideas; they are the commands of God in His Word.

The scriptures remind us it is not our job to get revenge. This is God's work and God's work alone. It is a sin against God to take His work as our own, to take things into our own hands. God's way is to manage conflict by managing rightly your urge to have revenge during or after the conflict. God could not be clearer. When you are in conflict, just resist the inner urge to return hurt for hurt. Don't return harsh words with harsh words. Don't respond to a push with your own push or a slap with your own slap. Just don't retaliate!

Personal Questions to Consider:

Do I feel I want to take vengeance on anyone for what they have done to me in conflict?
Do I wish anyone harm, either physically, mentally, or emotionally when we are in conflict?
When in conflict, do I return hurt for hurt, therefore keeping the hurt cycle going?

Word Six

We Are To Work toward Peace

1 Cor. 14:33 *For God is not the author of confusion, but of PEACE.*

Prov. 16:7 *When a man's ways please the LORD, he maketh even his enemies to be at PEACE with him.*

Matt. 5:9 *Blessed are the PEACEmakers: for they shall be called the children of God.*

Mark 9:50 *Salt is good: but if the salt have lost its saltness, wherewith will ye season it? Have salt in yourselves, and have PEACE one with another.*

Luke 1:79 *To give light to them that sit in darkness and in the shadow of death, to guide our feet into the way of PEACE.*

Eph. 4:3 *Endeavouring to keep the unity of the Spirit in the bond of PEACE.*

Col. 3:15 *And let the PEACE of God rule in your hearts, to the which also ye are called in one body; and be ye thankful.*

James 3:17 *But the wisdom that is from above is first pure, then PEACEABLE, gentle, and easy to be entreated, full of mercy and good fruits, without partiality, and without hypocrisy.*

James 3:18 *And the fruit of righteousness is sown in PEACE of them that make PEACE.*

1 Pet. 3:11 *Let him eschew* (avoid strongly) *evil, and do good; let him seek PEACE, and ensue* (pursue) *it*

Author's Commentary

WOW! God puts a high premium on this thing called peace and those who work to bring peace. If there were ever two opposites, they would be "conflict" and "peace." Peace is much like unity; neither peace nor unity is guaranteed when people live, work, or even worship together. Although it may be difficult to secure peace in the midst of conflict, it is the Christian's duty to seek after peace and make peace with others whenever possible. Every Christian should want to be a peacemaker and exhaust all possible energy toward making peace.

Don't we all long for peace in life? Wouldn't a marriage full of peace be desired since half of all marriages end in conflict and divorce? Probably half of the other half of marriages experience conflict and battles. Wouldn't it be wonderful if we all fought for peace in our marriages?

That's true in the workplace and in the local church. Whenever conflict arises, each of us should heed the instructions of God and "wage peace" not war. Rather than fighting to get our way or win for our side, let's work just as hard to find ways to make peace our goal and our ultimate destination.

Personal Questions to Consider:

Am I a person of peace?
Do others see me as a person who is working hard to bring about peace or as a person determined to win every battle?
Am I willing to be at peace, even when I don't get my way?

Word Seven

Recognize the Role Satan Plays in Conflict

1 Pet. 5:8–9 *Be sober, be vigilant, because your adversary the devil, as a roaring lion, walketh about, seeking whom he may devour. Whom resist steadfast in the faith...*

Eph. 4:27 *Neither give place* (opportunity) *to the devil.*

Eph. 6:11 *Put on the whole armor of God, that ye may be able to stand against the wiles* (schemes) *of the devil.*

2 Cor. 2:11 *Lest Satan get an advantage of us, for we are not ignorant of his devices* (methods he uses).

1 Tim. 3:7 *Less he fall into reproach and the snare* (trap) *of the devil.*

Gal. 5:19 *Now the works of the flesh are manifest...hatred, strife* (conflict), *wrath* (anger), *dissentions* (arguments), *selfish ambitions* (desiring only your way).

James 3:14–15 *But if you have bitter envying and strife* (conflict) *in your heart...this wisdom* (way of thinking) *does not descend from above* (from God) *but is earthly...devilish* (of the devil).

then in 4:7b *Resist the devil and he will flee from you.*

Author's Commentary

Not all who disagree with you or me are evil people nor are they always led by the devil. We should not demonize any and all opposition. We often do so in order to feel we are on the side of "right" and therefore should prevail in the conflict. This will usually work against effective resolution of conflict.

With that said, we also must admit that some people may be influenced by the devil. Satan, the devil, the evil one does exist. Jesus spoke often of him, and the New Testament writers were also led of God to warn us of the part he plays in conflict situations. Let's again look at what God has to say.

The Bible says Satan is your adversary. He is against God, and therefore against you, against your marriage, against your successful work, and against your church.

He is out to get you anyway he can. He is stalking around every area of your life. He is setting snares or traps for you. He is scheming to tempt us to live in the flesh and produce the works of the flesh such as anger, strife, arguments, and the other works of the flesh that conflict can produce.

But we don't have to let him ensnare us. We can stand against him, resist him, know his ways, and his tricks. We should not give him any opportunity to ensnare us or to use conflict to trick us into acting in a fleshly, unchristian way. Remember, greater is He that is in you than he that is in the world. You have the power to choose how you act! You can resist his temptation and avoid his traps.

Learn to see him as he sets traps in your marriage and family. Those things that cause arguments and conflict in your marriage may be the devil's traps. My wife and I have learned after these forty-eight years of marriage that the devil loves to get us into conflict. We have learned the skill of turning the devil away by remembering what's really important. We see the devil almost daily setting his traps, and we simply step around them. We now know his ways and his schemes. We know our weaknesses and how he uses them to ensnare us in conflict. We then turn our guns on him rather than on each other.

It's the same in our local church. Satan is always setting traps for the church family. He wants us in conflict. He wants us to act badly and speak harsh words. In all those conflicts churches get involved in, we should ask God whose side He is on. And most of the time He would respond, "I don't care" and "What difference does it make in the real Kingdom work?" We argue about so many things that just don't really matter. The color of the new carpet, whether we need a new piano or not, what the proper start time is? Ninety percent of the church fights I've observed were about "stupid stuff." It was just the snare of the devil to neutralize or destroy our church.

We must learn to recognize the traps and snares of the devil which draw us into conflict. Then we can avoid or manage our conflicts in God's way.

Personal Questions to Consider:

When in conflict, do my ways indicate I am under the influence of Satan?
When in conflict, do I exhibit the works of the flesh such as anger, wrath, revenge, strife, and dissention?
When in conflict, do I let down my guard and defenses against Satan's influence in my life?
Do I watch for and avoid the traps Satan sets or am I easy prey for him?

Word Eight

Judging Others Is Wrong and Forbidden

Matt. 7:1–2 *JUDGE not, that ye be not JUDGED. For with what judgment ye JUDGE, ye shall be JUDGED: and with what measure ye mete, it shall be measured to you again.*

Rom. 2:3 *And thinkest thou this, O man, that JUDGEST them which do such things, and doest the same, that thou shalt escape the judgment of God?*

Rom. 14:13 *Let us not therefore JUDGE one another anymore: but judge this rather, that no one put a stumbling block or occasion to fall in his brother's way.*

1 Cor. 4:5 *Therefore JUDGE nothing before the time, until the Lord come.*

> **James 4:12** *There is one lawgiver, who is able to save and to destroy: who art thou that JUDGEST another?*

> **Rom. 14:4** *Who art thou that JUDGEST another man's servant? To his own master he standeth or falleth. Yea, he shall be holden up: for God is able to make him stand.* **14:10** *But why dost thou JUDGE thy brother? Or why dost thou set at nought thy brother? For we shall all stand before the judgment seat of Christ.*

Author's Commentary

To judge someone is to condemn that person. This judgment is usually accompanied by a hateful attitude and ill feelings toward the person being judged. We often pass judgment on a person or group of persons we are in conflict with at any given time. God tells us in His word that this is His work, not ours. We are each sinners and that disqualifies each of us from judging others. We are to observe the actions and words of others in an attempt to rightly relate and rightly minister to others. We know people better by observing them. It is true that we are to be proclaimers of the Word of God and speak in love the truth found in God's word. We are to admonish, to teach, to proclaim, and even rebuke a fellow Christian who is in sin. The Holy Spirit is the one who does the convicting but He does it through the Word of God being communicated by other Christians. The problem arises when we erroneously see ourselves as better than others and have our own personal, and many times distorted, understanding of what a person or a Christian should be like. The problem arises when we see ourselves as spiritual police who are to blow the whistle whenever we think someone is not in line with our understanding of the "right way." We often become "circle checkers" in that we super-impose our "Christian circle" over the Christian circle of others and judge or condemn them when their circle is out of line with ours. God used Paul in Romans 14 to caution us not to be judgmental and condemning of others in doubtful or gray areas, areas where there is wide spread differences of opinion as to right and wrong. Our instructions to others must be true to God's Word and not just our opinion and judgment. God tells us it is not our job; He will handle it as the righteous judge in His own time. The damaging attitude that comes with our judgment of others hurts our attempts at resolving conflict.

This judging attitude and words often include deciding in our own mind what a person's motive is for any word or deed or position. It is really impossible to know a person's heart or motive. We cannot know what a person's motive is, unless they tell us. To prejudge a person's heart or motive is to take on a role reserved only for God. Often in the heat of conflict, we jump to judge the opposition's motives, and we are really incapable of this. We may be right, and we may be wrong. To do so wrongly is to bear a lying witness about someone else, and we all know that to be wrong in God's eyes. You really only guess when you tell your spouse he or she did or said something with a particular motive. To say your boss did something with a secret motive is to chance being wrong. To believe or to say your pastor, a deacon, or church member said or did something with a definite motive is to only guess it is so. To judge this and do it as an imperfect sinner yourself is to venture into the realm where only God can go. The next chapter will shed more light on this important subject of being judgmental. God tells us to resist the urge of judging others we are in conflict with, if we want to manage conflict His way.

Personal Questions to Consider:

Am I judgmental of someone I'm in conflict with?
When in conflict, do I look for faults in others that I can use to win the conflict?
Have I passed judgment on someone else's motives?
Do I talk critically of others behind their back without talking to them?
Do I give as much attention to my own sins as I do the sins of others?

Word Nine

Be Tolerant of Differences

Rom. 14:3 *Let not him that eateth despise him that eateth not; and let not him which eateth not JUDGE him that eateth:* (it would be good to read all of chapter 14 to get the message here).

Author's Commentary

Christians are to be true to "Biblical truth," but we also should be careful not to become intolerant of those who have different opinions about things that are not clearly and definitively spelled out in scripture. The example of this passage from God's Word is right on the borderline of right and wrong in the eyes of believers in those days. There are many conflicts that revolve around right and wrong and the gray area between the two. We love to be right and to be on the side of right. We can get in great conflict as they did in this passage where the true right and wrong can be somewhat unclear. God is telling us to err on the side of tolerance and unconditional love when the matter of the conflict is "doubtful" or unclear.

Whether in marriage, church, or elsewhere, we are to be careful that our personal preferences don't become the "law of the land" or seen to be the "truth of God." Whether my spouse uses paper towels or a rag to dry out the sink is not worth "arguing" about. Whether your husband cuts his grass like you would is not an issue worth debating. My way of doing things will not always match everyone else's. The music or dress code or sermon length or a thousand other things may not be the way I prefer at my church, but it's not about just me. My convictions about things may be wrong or half true. I may be basing my position on false information or false understanding of things, or of Christian scripture.

It is not about getting everything done or said the way I think is best or right. I may have opinions and preferences, some even based on my interpretation of scripture, but I am to be tolerant and respectful of those whose opinions and preferences differ from mine. We do not have to all think alike to get along. A wife or husband, a family member, a fellow church member, a co-worker may do something differently. They may think outside my comfort zone, and it is still okay. We should stop demanding your way and start getting alone with others as God instructs us.

Let's think about several illustrations of how this intolerance of differences can increase the conflict in our everyday lives. Your spouse may believe one church is better than another or one version of the Bible is better than the other but intolerance can cause conflict. You think people should dress a certain way in church, and your spouse thinks differently from this. You are very sure the church should start at ten AM, but your good friend says it's okay to change the start time to nine AM. Your spouse thinks the trash goes out daily, and you think it should go out when it's full. You think it's wrong for women to wear women's slacks to church, and your best friend thinks that's okay. On and on the differences go, yet none of these issues are clearly addressed in God's Word. Many times our traditions become the "law" for us, and we aren't tolerant of any other views or opinions or interpretations. Be careful and tolerant in the gray areas of life and stay true to the black and white; learning to wisely know the difference.

Personal Questions to Consider:

When in conflict, do I always think others should think like I think?
When in conflict, does my attitude sound like "It's my way or the highway?"
When conflict is possible, do I take time to ask myself, "Does this really matter that much?"
Do others see me as a person who always thinks I'm right?
Am I seen as a tolerant or intolerant person?

Word Ten

Forgive Those Who Wrong You in Conflict

Eph. 4:32b *Forgiving one another, even as God for Christ's sake hath forgiven you.*

Luke 17:4 *And if he trespass against thee seven times in a day, and seven times in a day turn again to thee, saying, I repent* (I am sorry and I won't do it again); *thou shalt forgive him.*

Luke 6:37c *Forgive, and ye shall be forgiven:*

Matt. 6:12 *And forgive us our debts* (sins against others), *as we forgive our debtors* (those who sin against us).

Matt. 6:14 *For if ye forgive men their trespasses, your heavenly Father will also forgive you*:

Matt. 6:15 *But if ye forgive not men their trespasses, neither will your Father forgive your trespasses.*

Author's Commentary

One of the main themes of God's message in the Bible is that of forgiveness. We are told over and over of the importance of forgiving others. How many times does God have to say something for us to take it to heart and make it our way of life? We have been amazed over these nearly fifty years of ministry how many Christians ignore the clear teaching of Christ simply because it doesn't benefit them.

Forgiveness is not something we give an innocent person. Forgiveness is what we give the guilty person, the person who has wronged us. God says we're to forgive others just as Christ has forgiven us. God forgives each of us and in forgiving, He restores the relationship. He does not forgive and then tell us He doesn't want to have anything to do with us. When I forgive someone, I am to restore the relationship. My forgiveness is meant to make it as if the offense never took place. So many spouses can't forgive the hurt from the last conflict in the marriage. So many church members or ministers can't forgive the hurtful words said to them in a time of conflict. It's as if the words of God and the words of our Lord are tossed out the door because we don't want to obey. I guess it should not surprise any student of Christian scripture. In the Old Testament, God's people were so ready to forget God's commands whenever they seemed inconvenient. They were like us who disobeyed God over and over. We just can't see how we do it so often and feel so righteous in doing so. At least, they often repented and fell on their faces in regret over their sin. But we have lost the art of repentance and never see the error of our ways. We guess it's a matter of maturity. The mature Christian is submissive to God's commands even when they are hard. What confuses us most is that much of the time those who can't forgive are those who are supposed to be the most spiritual and mature.

The Bible says our forgiving others is the evidence that we ourselves have been forgiven. It should be the natural response of forgiven people to forgive others. What does forgiveness really mean? Our forgiveness, if it is to be as God's forgiveness, is undeserved. We can't wait for the other person to deserve of forgiveness. Our forgiveness does not depend on others. It comes out of the love and grace expressed to us by God, and that forgiveness flows to others through us. God's kind of forgiveness is removing the sin from us and treating us as if it had never happened. He restores the relationship when the forgiveness is given. For us to be truly forgiving of others, we must forgive when it is not deserved. The objective of forgiveness is to restore the relationship with that person. Forgiveness, in its purest sense, is to dismiss the fact that the transgression ever happened. For a husband or a wife, real heartfelt forgiveness would mean putting the offense in the past and restoring the marriage to the way it was before the offense. For two neighbors, it would be the same. If the conflict is within a church congregation, where forgiveness is supposed to be a way of life, the forgiveness would also restore relationships to pre-conflict peace and cooperation. This kind of forgiveness may seem wrong and even impossible to you, but we ask you to study the Word of God and decide if we are wrong or right in the true results of forgiveness.

This seems, to human terms and logic, to be impossible, but with God's help we can express this kind of forgiveness, even to those with whom we are conflicted. This is sometimes the only way to end conflict because the harm or hurt is already done and the only choices are retaliation and revenge or forgiveness and the resulting peace. Without the willingness to forgive, people are left with separation or divorce, ongoing hostility across the fence, or severe damage or the splitting of a local church congregation.

When conflict rages anywhere, God says we include forgiveness in the actions we take. To forget or ignore this word from God is to engage in conflict without the help and direction of God. How tragic.

Personal Questions to Consider:

Have I forgiven those who have done me wrong?
Do I forgive even when it's not deserved?
After I forgive, do I continue to condemn or reject the ones I have forgiven?

Do I openly admit I too have done things for which I need forgiveness?
Do I accept the forgiveness others give me and allow it to bring peace to the relationship?

Word Eleven

God Forbids Malice and Bitterness

1 Cor. 5:8 *Therefore let us keep the feast* (this could mean "gather as Christians for worship and fellowship"), *not with old leaven, neither with the leaven of MALICE and wickedness; but with the unleavened bread of sincerity and truth.*

1 Cor. 14:20 *Brethren, be not children in understanding: howbeit* (how can it be) *in MALICE be ye children, but in understanding be men* (mature).

Eph. 4:31 *Let all bitterness, and wrath, and anger, and clamour, and evil speaking, be put away from you, with all MALICE:*

Col. 3:8 *But now ye also put off all these; anger, wrath, MALICE, blasphemy, filthy communication out of your mouth.*

Titus 3:3 *For we ourselves also were sometimes foolish, disobedient, deceived, serving divers* (different) *lusts and pleasures, living in MALICE and envy, hateful, and hating one another.*

1 Pet. 2:1 *Wherefore laying aside all MALICE, and all guile, and hypocrisies, and envies, and all evil speakings…*

Heb. 12:15 *Looking diligently lest any man fail of the grace of God; lest any root of BITTERNESS springing up trouble you, and thereby many be defiled;*

James 3:11 *Doth a fountain* (inner self of a person) *send forth at the same place sweet water and bitter?*

James 3:14 *But if ye have BITTER envying and strife in your hearts, glory not, and lie not against the truth* (Don't lie about how you feel).

Author's Commentary

God's Word says we're not to have malice or bitterness, spite or ill will toward others. We must not forget or just ignore this when the emotions involved in conflict begin to set in.

The word '*malice*' carries with it the meaning of inner evil feelings about others. This ill will toward others can cause us to act in an unchristian manner. This malice can cause us to ignore all the instructions we have pointed to in this book. Our malice becomes the motivator rather than the actual issues of the conflict. Before we can act in a Christian way toward others, we must search our own hearts as to our emotions and feelings toward others. It is important that we do not justify our ill will, our malice, by the fact that someone or some group has hurt or gone against us.

Then there is the human tendency toward bitterness God addresses in His word. Adrian Rogers described bitterness as "an acid that destroys its own container." A good friend and co-worker in the ministry, Eric Boykin, points out in a recent article on bitterness, that in 1 Samuel 18–22 bitterness poisoned Saul's leadership, his relationships, and his worship. Bitterness is indeed a poison acid that can destroy you in many ways.

In a way, bitterness is like unkindness. It is hard to recognize, especially in our own lives. Bitterness is also hard to define, but if you are honest, you know when bitterness is present. Let's try to understand this thing God calls bitterness. Bitterness is an inner feeling of anger and resentment toward another person or group. God says a very small root of bitterness can grow to be a terrible presence in your life. We hope each of us knows when we feel bitter toward another person. We should examine our hearts to make sure that these feelings of bitterness are not present. It is important that conflict be based on facts and evidence rather than our emotions which are distorted by the conflict. If we find bitterness in our lives, we should prayerfully search the Scripture and seek God's help in replacing this bitterness with love, patience, and forgiveness.

Personal Questions to Consider:

Do I have malice or ill will toward anyone when I'm in conflict with them?

Do I understand that to have malice is to act in a way God calls childlike?

Do I understand that malice is listed with many other sins which a Christian is to avoid?

Is there any bitterness in my life right now…toward anyone or toward any group?

Will I listen to God's Word and put malice and bitterness out of my life?

Word Twelve

Patience Is God's Way, Even in Conflict

2 Pet. 1:5–9 *And beside this, giving all diligence, add to your faith virtue; and to virtue knowledge; And to knowledge temperance; and to temperance **patience**; For if these things be in you, and abound, they make you that ye shall neither be barren nor unfruitful in the knowledge of our Lord Jesus Christ. But he that lacketh these things is blind, and cannot see afar off, and hath forgotten that he was purged from his old sins.*

Titus 2:2 *That the aged men be sober, grave, temperate, sound in faith, in love, in **patience**.*

1 Tim. 6:11 *But thou, O man of God, flee these things; and follow after righteousness, godliness, faith, love, **patience**, meekness.*

Rom. 15:5 *Now the God of **patience** and consolation grant you to be likeminded one toward another according to Christ Jesus:*

1 Thess. 5:14 *Now we exhort you, brethren, warn them that are unruly, comfort the feebleminded, support the weak, be **patient** toward all men.*

1 Tim. 3:3 *Not given to wine, not striker, not greedy of filthy lucre; but **patient**, not a brawler, not covetous;*

2 Tim. 2:24 *And the servant of the Lord must not strive; but be gentle unto all men, apt to teach, **patient**.*

Gal. 5:22–23 *But the fruit of the Spirit is love, joy, peace, longsuffering* (**patience**), *gentleness, goodness, faith, meekness, temperance* (self-control).

Eph. 4:2 *With all lowliness and meekness, with longsuffering* (**patience**), *forbearing* (putting up with) *one another in love;*

Col. 3:12 *Put on therefore, as the elect of God, holy and beloved, bowels of mercies, kindness, humbleness of mind, meekness, longsuffering* (**patience**);

2 Tim. 4:2 *Preach the word; be instant in season, out of season; reprove, rebuke, exhort with all longsuffering (**patience**) and doctrine.*

Author's Commentary

Don't we all need more patience? One of the hardest things in life is to be patient with others, especially when we are engaged in conflict. We believe it must be that our desire to have things our way makes us so impatient with others. This means that impatience is a sign of selfishness, and we've already shown that selfishness is not a characteristic of God-like love. It is not to be the way Christians think or act. This is true always, but it can help us not only avoid conflict but it also helps us resolve conflict. Selfishness can wreck a relationship, a marriage, a church, or your lively-hood. It is important that we be patient in our dealings with other people with whom we find ourselves conflicted. God's Word makes it clear we are to be patient with our brothers and sisters in Christ. This word from God is not cancelled out when we are in conflict in the church. Patience will change everything as you relate with your husband or wife. This is true across the neighborhood fence and the desks at the office or on the assembly line.

Remember how patient God is with each of us. God expects the same patience from us as we relate to others. Did you notice how huge the number of scriptures where God calls us to patience? When we are frustrated by the actions or words of others, we should pause in a patient spirit and take time to consider all the factors involved. We should give others the time they may need to think, to progress in their thinking, to come around in their understanding of the situation. Patience does not press or hurry another person or group. This is the beginning of patience; not to react quickly, but to prayerfully consider our reaction to others. This is the safeguard against acting out of emotions. Patience keeps us from putting our mouth and even hands into motion before we have time to put our brain, and our heart, into gear. Let us be patient with those we are in conflict with, giving the Lord time to work in their lives also.

Personal Questions to Consider:

Am I a patient Christian?
Do others see the fruit of patience in my life?
Am I patient with everyone, even those who disappoint me?
When I correct someone, do I do it patiently?
Do I pressure others to quickly do it or see it my way?
When in conflict, do I forget to be patient?

Word Thirteen

The Greatest of these is Love

Prov. 10:12 *Hatred stirreth up strifes: but love covereth all sins* (hides or dismisses transgressions).

Matt 5:44 *But I say unto you, love your enemies, bless them that curse you, do good to them that hate you, and pray for them which despitefully use you, and persecute you;*

1 Cor. 13:4, 8 *Love suffereth long, and is kind; love envieth not; love vaunteth not itself, is not puffed up, love never faileth:*

Rom. 12:9 *Let love be without dissimulation* (hiding the truth).

Rom. 12:10 *Be kindly affectioned one to another with brotherly love.*

Rom. 13:10 Love *worketh no ill to his neighbour: therefore love is the fulfilling of the law.*

1 Thess. 4:9 *But as touching brotherly love ye need not that I write unto you: for ye yourselves are taught of God to love one another.*

1 Tim. 6:11 *But thou, O man of God, flee these things; and follow after righteousness, godliness, faith, love, patience, meekness.*

1 Pet. 1:22 *Seeing ye have purified your souls in obeying the truth through the Spirit unto unfeigned* (sincere, not pretended) *love of the brethren, see that ye love one another with a pure heart fervently:*

1 John 2:10 *He that loveth his brother abideth in the light, and there is none occasion of stumbling in him.*

1 John 3:10 *In this the children of God are manifest, and the children of the devil: whosoever doeth not righteousness is not of God, neither he that loveth not his brother.*

1 John 4:20 *If a man say, I love God, and hateth his brother, he is a liar: for he that loveth not his brother whom he hath seen, how can he love God whom he hath not seen?*

1 John 4:21 *AND this commandment have we from him* (Jesus), *that he who loveth God, love his brother also.*

Author's Commentary

Out of all the Christian virtues, love is supreme! God Himself is LOVE. The Word of God, which we all say we love and seek to obey, tells us that God is love and those who know God will know His love and express His love to others. This means our spouse, our boss, our employees, our pastor, our deacons, our church members, everyone. This love command applies to our enemy, those who hate us, those who hurt us, those who don't agree with us, those who oppose us, and on and on go the people of whom this call to love applies. Scripture is very clear that this love is not a "feeling." It is the "way we act" toward others. This is so important! I may not feel loving toward someone or some group, but I must act in loving ways toward these people. I must do loving things. I must speak in loving words. Even when I'm opposing them or when I'm setting them straight, I must speak truth in love. As I pointed out earlier, even my words must be said with love as my motive and in a loving way.

Think what that would do in those marital arguments and conflicts. Think how different those church conflicts would sound. To be truly Christian is to hear and obey these commands of our Father and of the Lord, and to do it even when it's hard.

The evidence of the presence of God's Holy Spirit in our lives is that we have love for others. That's why love is listed as the fruit of the Holy Spirit living within each of us. Paul makes it clear that love is patient and kind and humble and forgiving…even when we are in conflict with others. That love must change the way we act. It must change the way we respond to the words and actions of others. Remember, these are not our words or ideas but those of God Himself.

God's Word says the absence of this love causes everything else in a Christian's life to be of little meaning to God. Without love, we are nothing more than empty sounds. No matter what's happening around us, or to us, let us truly express the love of God to everyone, even those involved in our conflicts.

Personal Questions to Consider:

Does my love cover the sins of others…helping me refuse to tell others about their sins (transgressions and hurts against me)?
Do I love those I consider my enemy, those who oppose me?
Does my love for others show openly, even to my enemies and those who oppose me?
When in a conflict, do I speak my words with a loving motive?
When in conflict, do I speak in a loving way?
In conflict, do I say words that reflect disgust, harm, and hate, rather than love, toward those who oppose me?

Word Fourteen

We Are to Safeguard Unity and Oneness

First, here are scriptures about unity and oneness among fellow Christians:

> **Phil. 2:2** *Fulfill ye my joy, that ye be likeminded, having the same love, being of one accord, of one mind* (be unified through compromise or agreement).

> **Eph. 4:3** *Endeavouring* (work) *to keep the unity of the Spirit* (being unified with others who are Christians) *in the bond of PEACE.*

> **Acts 1:14** *These all* (all the Christians) *continued with one accord* (in agreement) *in prayer and supplication...*

> **Acts 2:1** *And when the day of Pentecost was fully come, they were all with one accord in one place.*

> **Acts 5:12** *And by the hands of the apostles were many signs and wonders wrought among the people; and they were all with one accord in Solomon's porch.*
>
> **Col. 3:15** *And let the peace of God rule in your hearts, to the which also ye are called in one body* (a body is unified, working together).

Secondly, here are scriptures addressing unity and oneness in marriage:

> **Gen. 2:24** *Therefore shall a man shall cleave* (firm hold) *to his wife and they shall be one flesh* (oneness).
>
> **Matt. 19:5, 6** *For this reason, shall a man leave father and mother and shall cleave* (work hard at holding close) *to his wife, they twain* (two) *shall be one flesh. Wherefore, they are no more twain* (two) *but one flesh. What therefore God hath joined together* (unified as one), *let not man put asunder* (cause to separate).

Author's Commentary

There are few things that harm the cause of Christ more than the loss of unity, whether it is in a marriage or in the family of God, the local church. The conflict we see in personal relationships in the neighborhood and the marketplace as well as in the workplace is also damaging to the cause of Christ when Christians are involved.

Jesus said the world would know we belong to Him when they see and experience our love for one another. This love is visible in our oneness and our unity. On the opposite side of that coin, the world will doubt we know Him when they see us without the love for one another that produces harmony and unity, in our homes, in our churches, and wherever Christians are found.

Unity and Oneness in the Marriage Relationship

In the marriage relationship, oneness is to be valued and protected. Our marriage vows usually include promises to be one and in harmony with each other as a show of our love. This love and the accompanying oneness should not be threatened or destroyed by words or deeds in conflict. When conflict arises in a marriage, both husband and wife should work to preserve the sense of unity and oneness, the sense they are on the same team working toward a solution to any and all conflicts.

When conflict arises in the marriage relationship, one of the goals should be to preserve the oneness and unity of the marriage. Too often husband and/or wife value more the winning of the argument and getting their way. The goal of most value should be compromise or solution that results in oneness and unity.

Unity and Oneness in the Church

In the church, the same team spirit should prevail as the oneness and unity is maintained. There is no way to calculate the harm done to thousands of church members, to the reputation of a local church, and to the mission of the church in general, when a church loses the ability to move forward in one accord. Often this unity and oneness is sacrificed over insignificant matters. Seldom is it over theological, moral, or ethical issues. Arguments and dissention normally arise out of a struggle for control and a desire to "have it my way." Often, it comes as the result of simple personality clashes or the preferences of the young versus the older or the traditional versus the contemporary. We often get in the middle of church conflict, and I think people often wonder which side God is on. The more church conflict I deal with, the more I realize the simple truth that God just doesn't care. It really doesn't matter to Him what color something is, or if the time of the services changes, or whether we use this hymnal or that hymnal. In the light of eternity and God's great work on this earth, ninety-nine percent of our petty conflicts just seem so insignificant. If God could get a word in when the conflict is raging, He often would say, "I don't care! Just work it out peacefully soon and get on with bigger, more important matters."

Every Christian's duty is to strive for oneness and unity within the body of Christ, His church. And it is HIS church, right? Too often we as Christians and church members try to possess what is not ours to possess. To control the church is to possess the church. But everything about the church and in the church belongs to the Lord. It is His church, not mine or yours. To sacrifice on the altar of "my way" the unity of the church is to commit a grievous sin.

We should guard this oneness in all the ways scripture reveals to us. There are many ways to express our feelings and insights without disrupting the oneness and unity of the church body. We must remember church is not about me and my preferences, but about God. Every Christian should be ready to compromise, tolerate, and work for agreement in the effort to protect the unity and oneness of His Body, the church. Let's be able to say in the end, we did all we could to keep the church, of which we are a part, in one accord.

Personal Questions to Consider:

Do I really want to live in unity with others?
Am I actively working to safeguard the unity of my marriage?
Am I being careful not to disrupt the unity of His church?
What concessions am I willing to make to preserve unity and oneness in my marriage?
Am I willing to compromise and tolerate in order to keep my church in one accord?

Word Fifteen

Observe All God's Submission Principles

God is a God of ORDER! He designs and plans out, in great detail, everything! He has given us a "book of instructions." It is a guide to all He has designed and put together. In those instructions, He sets up "submission guidelines" for all of His creation.

These guidelines include the relationships between mankind and the earth, citizens and government, slaves and masters (this could be looked at as employees and employers in today's world), children and parents, wives and husbands, and for Christians and their leaders or ministers. He goes on to honor the "submission" principle as He instructs all of us to be in submission to God and to each other in a spirit of humility. God often tells us of His high regard for humility or a humble person.

Let's listen to God speak about this divine order of submission and notice how it is designed to help us avoid and when unavoidable, manage and resolve our conflicts. Here are the passages that address these "submission" guidelines which should be considered as commandments by all Christians, even those dealing with conflict.

Creation Submit to Mankind

Gen. 1:28 *God blessed them, and God said unto them, Be fruitful and multiple and replenish the earth, and subdue it* (have dominion or control over it).

People Submit to King or Government

Matt. 22:21 *Render therefore unto Caesar the things that are Caesar's; and unto God the things that are God's.*

1 Peter 2:13–15 *Submit yourselves to every ordinance* (law or ruling) *of man for the Lord's sake… whether to the king as supreme…or to governors… for this is the will of God.*

Servants or Employee Submit to Masters or Employer

Then in **Vs. 18** *Servants, be subject* (submissive) *to your masters with all fear, not only the good and gentle, but also to the forward* (harsh).

In **Eph. 6:5,** again the same command is stated.

Children Submit to Parents

Eph. 6:1 *Children, obey your parents* (He goes on to tell fathers to treat children kindly, not causing wrath in them).

Wives Submit to Husbands

Eph. 5:22–25 W*ives, submit yourselves unto your own husbands, as unto the Lord…in everything… for the husband is the head of the wife* (God says this again in 1 Peter 3:1, and God goes on to tell husbands to treat wives in the right way and love them as Jesus loves the church and gave himself for her).

Church Members Submit to Church Leaders

Hebrews 13:17 *Obey them that have the rule over you* (some read "who lead you") *and submit yourselves, for they watch for your souls, as they who must give account* (to God) *that they do it* (Do what?… could be give account or could be lead you?) *with joy and not with grief: for that is unprofitable for you.*

And to Ministers God says in Peter 5:*2 Feed* (shepherd*) the flock of God…taking the oversight of* (serving as overseers)*…*vs. 3 says *neither as being lords over God's heritage* (those entrusted to you), *but being enamples* (examples) *to the flock.*

God goes on to say in 5:5, *young are to be submissive to the older and all are to submit to God, and we all are to be submissive to each other, in humility.*

Author's Commentary

It seems to me it's easy to see a pattern here. These principles of submission run throughout the Bible, and it seems clear to me that God is trying to bring order to this world, and to each of our lives. Following God's submission guidelines will make a tremendous difference in the way we handle conflict. It can also help us avoid conflict. Observing and seeking to live with these submission guidelines in mind can be preventative thinking when it comes to conflict.

Let's look at all these guidelines as to God's ideal planning of life under His control. Let's think about how God says we should relate to others and the impact this would have on the conflicts in our lives. The first guideline of submission is the one we found in Genesis. When God tells man to replenish the earth and subdue it, I believe it could be saying, "Bring it into submission." God is saying that the earth is to be in submission to mankind. This is only the beginning of the submission principles God gives us. The rest of these submission principles have direct application in helping us deal with conflict in several areas of everyday life.

God's Word tells us that citizens are to be in submission to the king or the government, whichever is the case. For most of us, this means I must obey the laws of the land, unless they are in direct contradiction to the Words of God. The only exception in scripture is in Acts where Peter gives us the words "I must obey God rather than man."

The third submission commandment or guideline has to do with slaves, and in our modern western world this could apply to employees, I believe. Slaves are to be in submission to their masters. As I said, in our time in history and in western civilization, this could apply to employees and employers. I as an employee, am to submit to my employer, obeying in humility. If the people I work for are instructing me to do or not do a certain thing, I should follow their instructions without conflict. I can discuss how I feel or present alternatives to their instructions, but when it comes down to a final decision, I must do what they say. God also states for us that this is true even if my master/employer is cruel or unjust.

Then God goes on to give instructions about submission of children to their parents. Children are to honor father and mother but God clarifies that this means children are to obey father and mother. How many family conflicts would be quickly resolved or even avoided all together if children were to obey this simple instruction from God. God knows if every person does what seems right in his or her mind, the result is naturally going to be conflict. Then once conflict arises, if every person still does what seems right to him or her, the conflict has no resolution. The conflict goes on and on as the emotions rise and the tempers flare. God knows there's no end with this system. So He gives us this guideline that states when parent and child are in conflict and no compromise is agreed to, the child must simply obey the parent. When the child grows up, then the child becomes the parent and bears the responsibility of being the final word, and the cycle continues as God planned it.

From there, God moves to the relationship between a wife and her husband. Please do not blame us for this biblical truth. If we had been in charge of these guidelines, I might have reversed this order and made it husbands be submissive to your wives. That would have made life a little better in my mind as a husband. But honestly, husbands would have the same resistance as some wives, children, slaves, and citizens. We were not in charge of these guidelines, and God was and is. He says wives should be submissive to their husbands. This submission should be seen as a submission to the Lord and includes every area of life. Some still insist this is wrong and surely an error of scripture. Some feel men and women are equal and they are right in that belief. But God's wisdom should be valued and obeyed. He lays out his plan of submission for the purpose of decision making and the resolution of conflict in the family and the marriage. Two heads is an invitation to unresolved conflict and unending arguments.

God carefully guards against abuse of this submission guideline when He goes on to command husbands to love their wives in the same way Christ loves the church. He gave Himself for her and treats her right. When differences arise and decisions must be made, a wise wife will trust into the hands of her husband the final decisions and gladly give him the responsibility for the results of those decisions. If the husband loves his wife and gives himself to her and for her, most wives would be glad to submit to that type of her husband's leadership. Without this command, the husband and wife fight for the control and the resulting conflict can damage the marriage relationship. The marriage and the family will experience constant battles as each one tries to lead and have things go the way he or she thinks best or more beneficial. How can we observe all his other submission commands and ignore this one simply because it is uncomfortable? All these areas of submission are given us for a reason and God's reasoning always seems to reflect His love for us.

The seventh submission guideline has to do with church, the scene of many a conflict. When you put dozens, even hundreds, of people together, you have the potential for many conflicts. So many different opinions and ways of doing things make for the ingredients of conflict. Many times those conflicts arise between the pastor and members of the congregation. But God's submission guidelines address the relationship between ministers and church members. The scriptures indicate pastors and other church leaders are chosen by God as leaders of the congregation, the people of God. These leaders care for the spiritual well-being of the congregation and will someday give a report as to how the congregation followed their leadership. Without followers, there can be no leadership. The resolve to follow the leadership of ministers, unless that leadership violates scripture, helps the church avoid conflict or resolve conflict once conflict arises.

Of course, leadership can be abused and misused. There are ways to deal with these abuses. It should be done in accordance with all the other Scriptures we have brought to your attention. Conflict over leadership within the church can be resolved in a way that will not destroy the ministry or the unity and effectiveness of the church. Church leaders who misuse or abuse their leadership authority, act morally or ethically wrong, or lead the church in an unbiblical direction should be addressed and corrected in a God-directed, God-honoring way.

As with husbands, pastors, and other ministers, as well as church leaders are given specific instructions as to how they are to lead and how they are to act. Good ministers usually find most Christians will follow their leadership. We will follow the leadership of our pastor and other church leaders unless it is clearly contrary to the Word of God. We will also feel free to express our ideas, insights, and spiritual revelations to them, but will follow their leadership after I have done so.

If conflict arises, we will act in a way that is in accord with the submission guidelines and the Words of God we have addressed in the book.

Finally, to conclude this matter of submission, let's remember we are all to be in a spirit of submission to God and to each other. God values highly those who are of a servant spirit and are humble in their dealing with others, even those we are in conflict with.

Personal Questions to Consider:

Do I know and obey God's guidelines of submission?

Do I rebel against those God tells me to follow?

Would obeying God's submission rules help me avoid or resolve conflict in my life?

As a minister God has put in a place of authority, do I submit to God and lead in submissive humility?

Word Sixteen

We Are To Think the Best of Others

Matt. 7:3 *And why beholdest thou the mote (splinter) that is in thy brother's eye, but considerest not the beam (log) that is in thine own eye?*

Phil. 4:8 *Finally, brethren, whatsoever things are true, whatsoever things are honest, whatsoever things are just, whatsoever things are pure, whatsoever things are lovely, whatsoever things are of good report; if there be any virtue, and if there be any praise, think on these things.*

1 Cor. 13:5 *Love…thinketh no evil;…believes all things, hopes all things."*

Author's Commentary

We have heard it said, "We should give the other person the benefit of the doubt." We believe the Word of God teaches us to do just that. If at all possible, think the best of the other person. You may be wrong about them, but it is better to err thinking the best than to judge someone wrongly or accuse someone falsely. Very often, conflict causes us to do just that. We think the worst because it helps us wage the conflict.

God's Word calls on us to think about the good in others and not let the negative stuff register with us. This seems too easy on others, right? Do unto others as you would have them do unto you! We must see ourselves as bad as others and others as good as we are. So when in doubt, give the other person, even your enemy, the benefit of the doubt. Christians should be the quickest to say "innocent until proven guilty". Our hearts should require evidence of the "worst" in someone before we assume the worst in them. When we are in conflict, we actually want to think the worst of our opposition so that we feel better in the assaults we conduct to win the conflict.

Each of us has a choice about how we look at others. We can choose to look as a hummingbird or a buzzard. It's interesting you can fly both of those birds over the same terrain at the same time. The buzzard will look for something dirty, rotten, and dead while the hummingbird will look for something that smells sweet and looks good. Each of us has a choice in life. We can either look at others through the eyes of a hummingbird or a buzzard. If we're looking for the bad, we can always find it. There is bad in everyone and everything. There is also good in everyone and everything. Let us resolve to look for the good in others and to let our love cause us to overlook the bad. You can always think the best of the other person if you choose.

Personal Questions to Consider:

Does conflict cause me to work harder to find fault with those who oppose me?
Do I give those who oppose me the benefit of the doubt?
Do I try to think the best about other people, even those who oppose me in some conflict?

Word Seventeen

God Says Love Even Your Enemy

Matt. 5:44 *But I say unto you, Love your enemies, bless them that curse you, do good to them that hate you, and pray for them which despitefully use you, and persecute you;*

Author's Commentary

Only one scripture? How many times must God say something before we take it seriously? This is a simple yet profound command, and it does apply to the way Christians conduct themselves during a time of conflict. We are called upon to love everyone, even our enemy. Those with whom we are in conflict can be seen as our enemy. We tend to consider the opposition more and more like our enemy as a conflict intensifies. This tendency can cause us to see our wife or husband as our enemy. It can cause us to see our pastor or the deacons or fellow church members as the enemy. Anyone who is in conflict with us can become in our minds our enemy. So what does it mean to "love our enemy?"

The New Testament explains what it means, and Jesus goes on to expand on the thought. He says we are to bless our opposition, our enemy. To bless is to hope the best for our opposition. He goes on to say do good things for your opposition and to pray for them. To love our opposition in this way would keep us calm and logical as we work through a conflict. Believe me, this is not the easy way. This is hard to do, but if you are able to see your opposition through these eyes, it will help you deal with conflict with far less pain and destruction.

We should remember that Paul in First Corinthians 13 explains that love is not something we feel toward others; rather it is the way we act toward others, no matter how we feel. God's Word says love suffers long; that means love is patient with other people. It says love is kind, as we addressed in an earlier section. It says this love does not act rudely and is not selfish. This means love does not demand its own way, regardless of the results. Not acting rudely may rule out screaming and hollering at your wife, your husband, your pastor, your church leaders or committees, your family member, or your boss. Love acts differently; love conducts conflict differently. It goes on to say love is not easily provoked. This means love does not have a short fuse and is not easily angered.

It goes on to say that love thinks no evil. The actual meaning of this verse is that love does not keep a record of the evil done to it. This means when others hurt us or do evil against us, our love for them keeps it from registering. We do not notice their actions. This love is so forgiving that it dismisses any perceived attack even as it happens. This kind of love will really change the way we go through conflicts. It says love does not rejoice in sin, but it does rejoice when the truth is known. It says love does not fail. If we have true, God-given love for others, that love will not disappear when others disappoint us, hurt us, or even work against us in conflict.

This does not mean we do not express how we feel or work hard to see things done in the way we believe they should be done. It does mean we never lose our love for others and that we conduct ourselves as those who love everyone, even our opposition in times of conflict. Love conquers all, and the greatest of all is love.

Personal Questions to Consider:

Do I express love to those with whom I disagree?
Do I regularly pray for those with whom I disagree?
Do I bless (want the best for) those I disagree with or see as against me in a conflict?
Do I do good things or bad things to those with whom I disagree and have conflict?
When I speak the truth as I know it, do I do it in love?

Word Eighteen

Exhibit Self-control in Conflict

Galatians 5:22–23 *But the fruit of the Spirit is love, joy, peace, longsuffering, gentleness, goodness, faith, meekness, temperance* (self-control).

2 Peter 1:5–6 *And beside this, giving all diligence, add to your faith virtue; and to virtue knowledge; and to knowledge temperance* (self-control).

James 1:26 *If a man among you seem to be religious, and bridleth* (control) *not his tongue, but deceiveth* (lies to) *his own heart, this man's religion is vain* (empty or meaningless).

and **3:3** *Behold, we put bits* (tools of control) *in the horse's mouths, that they may obey us; and we turn about the whole body.*

And **3:5** *Even so the tongue is a little member, and boasteth great things. Behold, how great a matter a little fire kindleth.*

Vs. **6** *And the tongue is a fire, a world of iniquity* (sin), *that it defileth the whole body, and setteth on fire the course of nature; and it is set on fire of hell.*

James 3:8–11 *But the tongue no man can tame; it is an unruly evil, full of deadly poison. Therewith bless we God, even the Father; and therewith curse we men, which are made after the similitude of God. Out of the same mouth proceedeth blessing and cursing. My brethren, these things ought not so to be. Doth a fountain send forth at the same place sweet water and bitter?* (We should make every effort to control our tongue.)

Prov. 16:32 *He that is slow to ANGER is better than the mighty; and he that ruleth* (controls) *his spirit* (himself) *than he that taketh a city.*

Author's Commentary

God sees a great need for temperance, and He calls for it over and over in His word. Temperance is self-control. The great need when we find ourselves in the middle of a conflict of any type is the need for "self-control." Whether it's at the workplace or at the church, or in our home or the neighborhood, self-control can make all the difference. Conflict brings out our dark side and when emotions flare, we say and do things we would not normally say or do.

God know us, and He knows the way to avoid bad decisions as to what we say and do is to be in control of ourselves, especially when we get into the heat and emotions of a conflict. Self-control is the decision we make to first think about things before we react. My spouse may say or do something that irritates me. I can react immediately or I can take the time needed to think about my best way of responding. My hasty response will be determined by my emotions at the time, but if I have self-control enough to think about my response, I may choose a better, more productive response. This is true at the workplace and in the church setting also.

This is why one fruit of the Holy Spirit living in us is self-control. We need it, better put, we need Him, to help us when the emotions call for hasty response. We all are tempted to act and re-act in the flesh, the way the "old man or nature" would; but self-control gives us the chance to choose the better way. Self-control gives us time to think about better responses and choose to re-act in the spirit, the way our new man or nature should act.

Self-control is important in every area of conflict, but it may be of the most value in the area of the tongue. When in conflict, it is our tongue, what we say, that has the capacity to make the conflict worse. In the James passages God gives us, He tells us the tongue is a fire. It is a destructive fire that spreads over everything. And isn't that the way the conflicts go? Most often conflicts are started by words, and conflicts enlarge and escalate with the words we say. Think back to the last conflict you had with your spouse, or your friend, or your co-worker, or a fellow church member. Weren't the words said the thing that really made the conflict worse and kept it from ending?

Often, it is our uncontrolled tongue that starts the conflict. You say something that hurts your spouse or friend. The words you said didn't really need to be said. You just let your mouth, or your horse as James 3 says, run wild and free, wherever and whatever the horse feels like. Your tongue running wild and free, not under careful control, will cause damage everywhere. Isn't it true with you as it is with me? We put our mouth in gear before we engage our brain or our heart. These words we say are powerful and cannot be put back in after they leave our tongue. Careless words that if you thought about them before you spoke them, you would have known the harm or hurt they would cause. Choose your words carefully to avoid starting unnecessary conflict. Control your words during a conflict in order to resolve the conflict.

This word about self-control may be the most valuable we have heard from God about how we act during conflict. Stay in control of yourself, especially when you are involved in conflict at any level. This self-control will give you the time to remember and listen and obey all the other words from God which we have given you in this book.

Personal Questions to Consider:

Do others see me as a person who has self-control?
Do I lose control of my emotions often?
When in conflict, do I re-act quickly to what people say or do?
Will I try my very best to let the Holy Spirit control me when conflict arises?

Word Nineteen

God Says We Should Live Unselfishly

1 Cor. 13:5 *"Love...does not seek its own way"*

Phil. 2:4 *"Let each one of you look out not only for his own interest: but also for the interest of others"*

Romans 15:1-3a *"We...are not to please ourselves. Let each of us please his neighbor for his good, leading to edification. For even Christ did not please himself..."*

1 Corn. 10:24 *"Let no one seek his own, but each one sthe other's will being"*

We know that many conflicts cannot be avoided. As we said in our introduction to this book, there are so many different ideas and opinions around us. Each of us is different, and we come from different backgrounds and experiences. Whenever we interact with others, it's only natural we have a clash of ideas, opinions, and personal preferences. So it's not always sinful to be involved in conflict. Sin comes into the picture when we allow the conflict to cause us to act in sinful ways.

But and that's a big BUT, we have come to realize through our own experience that most of the time our conflicts are brought about by our selfish nature. When we study our conflicts, most if not all revolve around our desire to have things our way. Just as anger usually revolves around our not getting something our way, conflict revolves around our desire and attempt to have everything our way. Think about that for a minute. Study your conflicts and see if that's true for you as well. In First Corinthians 13:5, God says real love considers the other person's wishes, desires, and preferences over its own. We can resist the sin of selfishness, the sin of wanting my way. WOW! Would this not reduce and resolve most conflicts if we stopped wanting our way all the time. I know a lot of people who seem to feel they are always right (human trait of our old nature, right?). People want things their way and will engage in conflict in order to force or at the least convince others.

A wife or husband wants to build a deck and the other spouse doesn't think it wise and doesn't want to do it. Two desires, two opinions of what's right to do. Only one can prevail, so the conflict rages on. If one were to live unselfishly about this issue, and give in, the conflict is resolved. The problem is no one likes giving in or giving up! We husbands need to heed the words of God where He says a husband must love his wife and give himself for her, as Jesus did the church. Our sinful nature is self-centered and selfish. God's Word tells us this again and again. Almost every conflict in our happy marriage has revolved around two people wanting different things. What if I simply resisted the inner urge to have it my way as often as I can? The more I do that, the less conflict arises. To hear my spouse's ideas or wishes and to honestly evaluate them, giving in whenever possible would solve a lot of our conflicts, right? Even in the area of sexual intimacy, where much marital conflict resides, each of us is instructed to give ourselves to our spouse anytime our spouse desires sexual intimacy. If my wife wants it, my unselfish response is to joyfully meet her needs. But my sinful old nature hates giving in. It hates giving in unless my new nature of love takes over and makes me love enough to actually enjoy giving in. Now, I should protect and do what's best for our life together and not give in when important things are at stake, but most of the time that's not the case. Most of the time it's just my personal desire or lack of desire that makes me resist being unselfish and giving. If I stay selfish, or she does, the conflicts rage on.

In all other areas of life, it works the same way. Someone might say, *"At my local church, I am often tempted to be selfish in that I want something done differently, done my way. Not handled correctly, this could be the birth of a conflict in my church. More tempting is the desire in a church conflict to demand my way and fight to see it so. The fact that the church isn't mine to control doesn't stop me. Even though the church is the Lord's, and He places leadership, often trained leadership, there to make decisions I think I know better. Even if my church votes on issues and decisions, I will become angry and combative if the vote doesn't go my way. It most often is a matter of insignificant importance and really only a matter of my personal preference, but I like my way to have sway over even the majority. I have even moved to a new church, several times."* This kind of selfishness is to be avoided if we live by the standards God gives us.

Selfishness and self-will is the cause of many a conflict and the reason many a conflict is not easily resolved. Put others first. Give in more often. Remember, life is not all about you. As a Christian, life is first about pleasing and following Jesus and then loving others sacrificially.

Personal Questions to Consider:

Am I seen by others as a selfish person?
Do I normally seek to have things my way?
How often have I given in over the past month or so?
Can I think of a single time I've given in to the other person's way
    or desire?
Could I help resolve some of my conflicts by just giving in?

Conclusion

We are all imperfect and fallible. We should all accept this truth about ourselves but never be so comfortable with it that we stop trying to improve. We should also tolerate imperfection and failure in others. We have all sinned and fallen short of God's glory. Most conflict revolves around sin and is made worse by ongoing sin. We should all seek to resolve conflict and make peace whenever possible. We should all seek to live in such a way as to avoid conflict if possible and manage it in a God-honoring way when it cannot be avoided. When in conflict, we must not forget, ignore or disobey what God has told us.

The following covenants can help each of us be strong in seeking the common good for everyone. They can remind us of God's words which will benefit our marriage, our livelihood, our friendships, our church, and the Kingdom of God on this earth. Consider signing one or all of these and encouraging others to do the same. Keep it in a special place where you see it regularly, like in your Bible, or on your desk. Read it again during times of conflict.

My Marriage Conflict Covenant

In light of the clear Word of God, I make a sincere covenant with Jesus and my spouse to conduct myself in accordance with His will when in conflict.

I will be a person of prayer, praying with an open mind and heart about issues that affect my marriage.

I will be true to His Word and to my personal convictions, and whenever these two contradict each other, I will obey the Word of God.

I will voice my convictions and opinions in a way that is proper according to God's Word.

I will humbly and respectfully express my opinions as opinions, realizing I am not all-knowing nor all-wise.

I will go to my spouse privately if I have a disagreement, before I talk to others about it.

I will seek to be in control of my words and actions so that I act and react in a Christ honoring way.

I will always strive to be kind, forgiving, loving, respectful, and exhibit the fruit of the Spirit and the characteristics of Christian love.

Signed _____

My Church Conflict Covenant

In light of the clear Word of God, I make a sincere covenant with my Lord Jesus Christ to conduct myself in accordance with His will.

I will be a person of prayer, praying with an open mind and heart about issues that affect my church life.

I will be true to His Word and to my personal convictions, and whenever these two contradict each other, I will obey the Word of God.

I will voice my convictions and opinions in a way that is proper according to God's Word.

I will humbly and respectfully express my opinions as opinions, realizing I am not all-knowing nor all-wise.

I will go to a person privately if I have a disagreement with that person before talking to others.

I will seek to be in control of my life in such a way that I act and react in a Christ-honoring way.

I will strive to be kind, forgiving, loving, respectful, and exhibit the fruit of the Spirit and the characteristics of Christian love even when in conflict.

When the opportunity presents itself, I will express and vote my prayerfully considered convictions. If a vote takes place, I will support the majority vote, believing it is the way God expresses His will for my church.

Signed _____

My Workplace Conflict Covenant

In light of the clear Word of God, I make a sincere covenant with my Lord Jesus Christ to conduct myself in accordance with His will.

I will be a person of prayer, praying with an open mind and heart about issues that affect my work.

I will be true to His Word and to my personal convictions, and whenever these two contradict each other, I will obey the Word of God.

I will voice my convictions and opinions in a way that is proper according to God's Word.

I will humbly and respectfully express my opinions as opinions, realizing I am not all-knowing nor all-wise.

I will go to a person privately if I have a disagreement with that person before talking to others.

I will seek to be in control of my life at work in such a way that I act and react in a Christ-honoring way.

I will strive to be kind, forgiving, loving, respectful, and to exhibit the fruit of the Spirit and the characteristics of Christian love even when involved in a conflict.

When the opportunity presents itself, I will express or vote my prayerfully considered convictions. If a decision is made, I will support the decision unless it violates God's Word, believing it is the way God expresses His will for my life.

Signed _____

Wall Display

GOD'S WORD ON CONFLICT

- Speak the Truth in Love
- Be Kind
- Cease from Anger
- Disagree in a Christian Way
- Do Not Retaliate
- Work toward Peace
- Recognize Satan's Role in Conflict
- Do Not Judge others
- Be Tolerant of Differences
- Forgive
- Avoid Bitterness and Malice
- Exhibit Patience
- Love Your Neighbor
- Protect Unity and Oneness
- Obey God's Submission Guidelines
- Think the Best of Others
- Love Even Your Enemy
- Stay In Control of Yourself
- Live and Act Unselfishly
- You may find it beneficial to record some words to yourself below:
- _____
  _____
  _____
  _____
  _____

About the Author

Jerry and Carole Wilkins have dealt with conflict for most of the 50 years they have been together. Jerry served 18 years as a Pastor in three states and for 28 years as a denominational leader. Carole worked on several church staffs and as a Biblical Lay Counselor, trained by the American Association of Christian Counselors. They have seen conflict in the church, the workplace, the family, and marriages. Carole provided free Biblical counseling to hundreds in several church counseling centers she established over a period of 14 years. Both she and Jerry have helped people, ministers, and churches manage every kind of conflict. They are serious students of God's word as it relates to resolving conflict and managing life.

Jerry and Carole have written about a dozen books and this is the fifth to be published thus far. Both Jerry and Carole write for local newspapers, magazines, appear on local radio and television. Between the two of them, they have worked with more than a hundred churches and spoken to dozens of conferences and seminars. Other books include Marketing Your Sunday School, Change Your Life by Changing Your Mind, A Practical Guide to Associational Missions, The Marriage Doctor, The Great Marriage Physician, Smooth Sailing, The Counseling Pulpit, and soon to be released Compel Them In.

The Wilkins are the proud parents of two grown children, David and Kimberly, as well as one granddaughter, Aly. They now enjoy retirement and more time together. They continue to serve Christ through their church and their writing ministry.

CPSIA information can be obtained
at www.ICGtesting.com
Printed in the USA
FSOW02n0635151016
26067FS